Overcomer: A collection of Original Poetry

Jess Fish

BookLeaf Publishing

India | USA | UK

Presentation by *BookLeaf Publishing*

Web: www.bookleafpub.com

E-mail: info@bookleafpub.com

ISBN: 9789360945855

First edition 2024

This book is dedicated to.... Me. I wrote this book for me. For me at 5 years old, so little with golden brown curly hair, so alone, so vulnerable. She has waited for healing and safety for the past 30 years. I am creating that world for her. I will save her. For a few years ago me when I fell off the ledge, coming to terms with trauma, anxiety, and depression. This was just a stop along the way and never was a death sentence or a life sentence. I am Overcoming. I am an Overcomer.

ACKNOWLEDGEMENT

I want to thank all of those that have offered me strength and support while I was struggling to just be alive. To my therapists and my family. Without you I would not be here. My therapists have been so adept at creating safe places for me to keep working on reigniting the light in my soul. i would not be here without the ultimate encouragement from my best friend and husband, Andy. To my three wonderful children that show me there is wonder in everything as well as humor.

PREFACE

Warning: some of these poems have content that includes domestic violence, suicide, and child abuse. This may be triggering to some readers. If you feel like I did, You feel hopeless and worthless and think that life is over for you. Get help. If you see someone acting differently. Address it. You can save a life. Call #988 for suicide. Contact your local behavioral health professionals, dial 911, and most importantly: Know that you are not alone and healing is possible. Tomorrow needs you.

My life has had it's unbelievable highs and equally life changing lows. I have struggled with complex PTSD for the past few years and this is a collection of poems from the middle of my journey. A journey to find purpose, self-love, self discovery, and healing. Working with some great therapists have definitely encouraged me to use art in ways to heal my soul. Since I have taken back up with my art including writing, I am finding myself. Not who I was but who I really am, authentically.

Making my Amends

I am a dichotomy of distressing distress.
I want to be a polished gem, a full-blown
success.
I have the tools; I know that I have been very
blessed.
I do not want to keep accepting less.
But,
Other parts of me thrive in the shadows
I do not want to cope with all these hard feelings
I am angry even rageful, I do not want to engage
with other human beings.
It is safer to be alone and hollow.
And,
I can drift off to my internal world of pain.
I can ignore what has happened.
Put the nightmares in a black trash bag and just
have memory gaps.
I have paid the price for my sadness; I own these
stains.
But,
When I look into my smoky green eyes in the
mirror.
God, it has been so long since I have been able
to do that.
I try to look past all the hurt and crap.

What is left? Am I a cold empty figure?
And,
I have let this go on far too long.
The mirror tells me no lies.
Unlike my brain's bias.
I whisper softly to myself; you must be strong.
So,
I am working on this plan.
Not like my plans in the past to quit or end it.
But a plan to repair my spirit.
I get out the tape, glue, and bands.
And,
I will keep working on it.
I have sweet little ones who are watching.
Thinking Mommy is there to do some
squashing.
Secure their safe place, squash their fear and
evicting the monsters from the closet.
So,
I go on. The love of my life is patient.
Waiting for me to be the girl he married
Though, I can only become a better version;
That me is buried.
He knows I am worthy to keep. To be
imperfectly the greatest.

Going to Tar

Laying out in the rain. My heart pains.
No one knows the cost. Wandering and feeling
so lost.
Running in the dark. I know that I have been
marked.
His long dark fingers possessing me, leaving
splinters.
Grabbing with long talons hunting as a black
falcon.
Swooping down in the night and then taking up
flight.
He wants a taste I am caught in his embrace.
I sense his hot breath on my shoulder, right
there, feeling an upcoming tear.
Instead, it burns. No one understands, it is my
turn.
The fire has claimed its victim. No one is
fighting this system.
A Cry, a sound so low, so sad, I must be bad.
The rain continues to fall, I am drowning in
alcohol.
I am fighting the reality of my own mortality.
Escaping even for a minute. I know no limit.
The monster hovers over me waiting lurking and
hating.
My light has dimmed. flickering with the roaring
wind

He lurches grabbing me from behind. I am out
of time.
His long hand and fingers stretch around my
neck, they linger.
The fingers stick to my skin grabbing me by the
chin.
Swirling, Stinking black smoke, I choke.
His body over comes my will. I will be killed.
Shaking and weak, my voice yells out, "no" yet I
have no choice.
The ominous black figure laughs as if to say this
has always been your path.
He puts his weight upon me and I am too late.
He starts to strangle me letting my limp body
dangle.
The black closes in and is growing, he whispers
in my ear, "we must be going."
My head hangs down and it starts to pound.
My breath gets short and shallow hanging in the
gallows
He says, "Your passing will bring no sad thing."
I draw my last breath and I meet my….. death.
I do not go up to the stars; I go down into the tar.
We have become one, welded together forever,
he has won.
My soul tangled in his long fingers. Rotten
breath lingers.
On my lips he whispers "mine" I knew this was
true the whole time.

The Favorite

I have always wanted to be a favorite.
For someone to ask "how have you been"
And really care about what was under my skin.
I always wanted to be a first round pick.
And not last like in high school gym class.
Being the one who everyone says "I'll Pass"
I have never been the first to know
Or had Someone's good news glow.
I am never the first to know someone's secret
plan.
Always feeling like a stunted left hand.
Or maybe a ghastly third wheel.
Pushing people away to numb the loneliness I
feel.
I want someone to love me the most.
One who will say "that's mine" and boast.
Not one who says "just stay in your corner."
As he finds a more comfortable shoulder
I hold in my loneliness and it sits on my chest a
heavy boulder.
No, I am not anyone's favorite girl.
I dream of love and romance twirled.
Instead, reality is that you and me never really
bonded.
An opportunity squandered.

I am not your special pearl found in low tide.
More like a clam shell tossed aside.
I am always the last to be told.
Never the one anyone wants to hold.
Maybe I am too just too cold.
Or I was born with an unlovable heart.
I know everyone will go away as I fall apart.
Eventually, they all do.
I just wish I could too.

Reborn

I feel the rush of my life passing
These feelings seem everlasting
The darkness can win again
All I hear is the ding.
Timer's up time to go,
I fall in tow.
I've been living in the shadows
Ruled by black and white rainbows.
On my chest lies the weight of the world
My life has become so whorled.
Spinning out of control
I cannot be consoled.
Quietly sitting on the bridge
This pain is too much, so is the rage.
Peering into the dark cold water
I can't be heard so I holler
God please stay away from me
I am irreparably destroyed
All your troops cannot be deployed
I am caught up in my misery
The water waits for its delivery.
I am standing on the side
I look up and sigh
Forgive me for being weak
This all seems so bleak

I am ready to fall
I should have attached a ball
And chain placed on my ankles
My thoughts continue to tangle.
Jump end it all
Answer the devil's call
Admit defeat.
My maker I will meet.
I deploy all my courage.
Flinging off the bridge
The outrage in my heart
I know it must depart.
Time moves by, a slow blast
But quick and fast
I know that this pain can't last.
I feel a release even a rush
My lungs are crushed
The crash of the cold
I have never been so bold.
I need to issue my plea
Will the water take me?
I have not been absolved I am here
My eyes begin to tear.
Another disappointing event.
In my heart is bittersweet regret.
I can't even kill myself right.
I know I must be like a kite.
Returning from whirling in the air
Reminding me life is never fair.

As if I needed to reminded
This pain had me so blinded.
I choose to continue to go on.
I can no longer be a pawn.
Lifting myself up from the water.
I will go on farther
We can at any point start again.
I may be a plain Jane
But have an underlying
Survived until the dawn
and it is no longer night
I still have time. I can try with all my might.

Counting On...

Between the light and the darkness
Hoping not to go down that slope.
Wishing for the sharpest hardness
A resilience only I can hope.

Choice, do we have a choice?
Darkness comes on easy
I try to silence that voice.
But all I feel is queasy.

Everyone else seems to be happy
I cannot feel. I am numb
Another day, I feel the trap.
God, I only feel like a bum

I can try to fight; I go on bended knee.
I know it's not right that I see the devil dance.
He's Coming for me, It is my last chance. You see
Into the future I am wearing my big girl pants

I fight for the light
I am tired and messed
I want to soar like a kite.
The past makes me so stressed

I say "I will get out of the dark"
I talk and talk and blurt
Igniting my life with a spark
And out with all the bullshit. sorry to be curt.
There is help for these wounds
While splashing out the crud.
I can climb out the tombs.
And out of the mud.

Like a warm smiling sun, now
A helper arises and practically glows
I do not have to always bow
The light now shows.

I can choose to stay
I can choose to live
I can begin again and not sway.
I have more to give.

I talk to you and you can
Talk to me always, without delays
I finally have a good safety plan
I no longer will count down the days.

Living present in the days ahead
I can do this and so can youw
I am building up tread.
We have hope to begin and start anew.

It hurts at first
But most hard things do
I finally feel no thirst
I can finally see more than blue.
Join me in this awakening!
Get down to business
Head and heart straightening
But, Who knows the distance?

Love and kind words to you
You are strong with such power
I know all that you can do.
Please do not cower.

Accept my condolences
But we can no longer just linger
We can improve our focuses
We will become much bigger.

Brave and strong
To continue the journey
Into the world we belong
And not out on a gurney.

You see I feel alright
I also want you to feel bright
I finally can accept the light.
I know the work feels right.

Do not make it the ending
We are just beginning.
I know it hurts from all the bending.
We can go on without all the spinning.

There is help you see
Call or text day, night or evening.
You can next do more than just flee
You can be all of your being.

Food, A Love Story

I continue to get more depressed and stomach
big,
Eating has become my full-time gig.
Gearing up now first meal of the day.
Eating breakfast to keep the bad feelings at bay.
Ah, short lived, I feel it. More anxiety has
arisen.
My body has become my prison.
The more that I eat the worse my feelings get.
The worse I feel the more I eat yet.
My protective layer has gotten out of control
With each and every over filled bowl.
Ice cream and sweets "Oh My"
I am committing slow suicide.
The drive is feeling full, which has never been
found.
I just continue to let myself drown.
I feel hopeless and confused.
My ego is very bruised.
The more and more that I eat
The feelings of worthlessness repeat.
Do I hate myself?
Is that the reason I take this cake off the shelf?
As I sit each day, with more food, the bigger I
get.

I wonder, Do I have any power over it?
In order to survive, we all must eat.
So why do I have this problem I cannot beat?
The questions swirl as another meal begins
I dig in and eat, the unsatiable hunger wins.
I know all the rules.
I have had the tools.
Instead, I hold close, my problem
Wondering, what will be my bottom?

The Forest

The sun can be shining. The rain may be
pouring.
This world restores me. Always changing and
inspiring.
Never do I feel or think more clearly, than when
I am in the woods.
My clouded mind never thought anything could.
Like I would always hurt so severely.
There is healing in the fresh dew. There is love
in every flower.
The trees they have special powers. They
whisper to me "there is always hope for you."
Walking through my worry goes away. I feel a
calm I have not felt.
I do not feel the shame of the hand I was dealt. I
know that I can make it through today.
Healing me from the inside out. I know that I
have nothing to fear.
I even let out a guilt free tear. I can mourn my
self-doubt.
New life begins to sprout. A life of new
steadiness wherever I steer.
Being whomever I choose. That is the key to a
life well lived.

Knowing that I do not want to be killed. It's
okay if I win or if I lose.
There is beauty in each dose. There is self-love
and joy available to me there.
Alone in the forest wandering as a mama grizzly
bear. I know I will get to acceptance and peace. I
speak loudly "Where is it?" Deep inside
answering, "you are so close."

Panic Attacks

Heart beats fast.
Ok, breathe, it's okay.
Hand to chest, quick
Breathe, Control it, Control it.
Breathe! faster.
Breathing in, out, in, out
inoutinoutin
I can't do this.
can't do this.
Mind racing.
Heart beats fast.
Skip Bom, bom, skip bom.
Hand to face. Cover Face
No one can see me
Like this. Messy
Embarrassed.
Who's looking at me?
Red face, Hot face
Breath quick in, and out.
Can't Turn off the world
World is loud
Mind racing
Won't stop racing
Shit. Stop. Just stop.
Can't do it.

Overwhelm.
Heart beats fast.
Skip beat, beat
Hand rubbing collar bone
Save me please
Hot sweat
Clammy hands
Choking on air
Cough.
Retching
Someone grabbing
Gasp, gasp.
Wheeze
Overwhelm
Skip beat, skip beat
Wheeze Wheeze
I hear yelling
Can't do this.
Down on knees
Heart beats beats beats.
Crash to the floor
Curl up. Breathe in breathe out.
Safe place: Camp warm breeze
Breathe, breathe, okokok
Lighten tension. Tear tear tear.

A Lovely Good-Bye

Young and free
Trying to climb all the trees
The warm summer air
Blowing through her long hair.
The sun kisses her skin
This is how her story begins.
Same as any other girl
Running with wispy bouncing curls.
She had such a light
It had shown so bright
It blinded birds in flight
Smiles, hugs, and kisses
Laughing in fields of flowers, making hand
whistles
The dark crept in slowly then all at once
She was marked by just five.
Kicking into mode: survive
She uttered not a squeak.
She knew better than to speak.
He went straight to work
 she was comforted by his smirk
Tickling and giggling
She was yelling, thrashing, and wiggling
Innocent to the eye
But no one knew the dark that was inside.

His hands did the travelling
And all the unraveling.
His heart was black
He did not care about what he lacked:
Moral code and control
Blues eyes found to be black
Would aways be on her to track
demanding she pay the toll
His hands did the creeping
Her heart was leaping
Out and Down to her feet
Keep quiet and do not repeat.
Her cheeks hot and burning red
She was sad and did not want to be on the bed.
She wanted to run away from the dark
but it was only the start.
Days and days, weeks, and years
No one noticed her tears.
She was a good girl and passed
But It was hard for her to be in class.
Her soul shattered forever
On that cold day in September.
Her body was claimed
And violently maimed.
She could no longer shine
And now always felt a threat from behind.
Good bye sweet little one
Your wonder is gone.
No one understands why you are no longer fun

She can no longer live her same happy life.
Knowing nothing but strife.
Who she was is destroyed
The darkness leaves a deep and dark void.
She will never have justice
because he always threatened "just us"
The way she began
Would never be her again.
She was different
Jaded and indifferent.
She gained a black figure, a black cloud
Living in shroud.
She knows this pain forever
Damaged by a push of a lever.
Good bye to you little girl
I know that you loved your dress to twirl.
And to Laugh in the sun
We will be together when I am done.
The Dark calls her close
But she wants a different course.
Life is a hard place.
What he wanted to chase
was her light, he possesses it for good
Knowing what she should do
Be quite reserved and never true
The first try, the cold night
Comes and she takes flight.
Leaving me to pick up her pieces.
Silently keeping the secrets as he pleases.

Boy Mom

Fire trucks, rocks, frogs.
I am a boy mom.
A Cackling Daredevil flailing down a hill.
I am a boy mom.
Yelling "Be careful"
Always watching and prayerful.
I am a boy mom.
Muddy, cheesy smiles.
I am a boy mom.
Dirty hand smudges on… everything.
Yup, I am a boy mom.

Being a boy mom is hard sometimes.
You sing a different song and rhyme.
Girls sit and cuddle.
Loving to stay in the momma bubble.
Boys are always on a dash.
But enjoy it now mama. Just laugh at all that
gas.
His long gangly legs and wild hair.
Remind me I have been there.
I've been there the whole time to witness
This boy transforming business.

Then, Girls, Video games, and cars.

I am a boy mom.
Gas money, late night calls, unanswered texts.
I am a boy mom.
Still getting hugs, check ins, and dad jokes.
Yup, I am a boy mom. Even still. Always will.

Serentiy

There is a special song that the flowers sing.
It is a blessing to be able to hear
It is a soft, complex sound, and can wipe away
fear.

I find myself basking in the calm that it brings.
I hear another song; it is a bee buzzing along

Between the leaves the brightness pokes
through.
The sun shining warmly on my face.
I rest. Knowing I am in a beautifully wonderous
place.
This must be where I belong.
I have been looking for this place all along.

For years, I have been spending my life on the
run
And finally, I am done.

I am ready to face my past, my weaknesses.
I calm. Laying in the deep soft green moss.
Strewn out on the floor of the forest.

Here, I may be just a tourist.

But I feel like, I want to be lost here.
Lost in a magical space.
A world I never knew but now a beautiful
embrace.
Where I can live by my own spirituality.
Without expectations so great.
While laying between the tall trees,
I am expected to do nothing. Be me and nothing
more.
No words must be spoken. No way needs to be
paved.
My eternal soul has been saved.

Revolution. I was merely chattel, always
needing to please others.
Control. But, no one has been worried about
how my heart bleeds.

But I want to take nature as my protector and
mother.
To be able to know myself well
So that when I am asked "who are you? Really"
I can easily tell.
Self-awareness will be something I will learn
first.

There is comfort in being alone among the
mighty timber

No one to think "Oh she is doing something so
weird."
Only alone my mind can be completely cleared.
My mind freed and flying, the soundtrack,
the forest's hauntingly beautiful timbre.

I am not Who I was Before

I am not who I was before. I will never again be
the same.
I am working on myself and trying to find what I
may gain.
I am fighting the darkness that has over taken
my brain.

For the first time, I am peacefully sleeping with
my back to the door.
The darkness follows me no more.
Because I threw him to the floor and out of the
door.
Instead of the being punished with regretful
spikes, I have taken up a soft warm blanket
feeling like nook reading in an old book store.

I am no longer the girl who always feels like she
has put on an act.
I am not fighting with the past and focusing on
what I lack.
I know, I will falter. It is a hard-fought journey
taking a life back.

The sun shines bright now and my air is crisp
and clear.

I know along the way that I will fight back more
fear and tears.
The weeping is cleansing me now making it
easier to cheer.

No, I am not the girl who got spooked when it
got hard. Then would flee.
I am a new sturdier version, facing it, as a strong
rooted tree.
I am not the same girl fighting to just be.

The light comes through the trees and lifts the
heavy air.
Peacefully wandering the earth as a mother
grizzly bear.
Both gentle and ferocious I stumble to balance
the pair.

I am not who I was, I am not the same.
I have changed and now, I play a different kind
of game.
This game now has both moments of hope, love
and inevitably pain.

There has been an explosion, an awakening of
sorts.
Keeping my eyes future looking, I know my old
ways I had to abort.

It is hard to get rid of it though, Like the burning
and returning of an unwanted wart.

No, I am not who I was with my depressed
reality blurred
Pain and hurt do subside and now I fly free like
a bird.
Putting trust into my own wings to bring me
forward.

Even though it may all burn, It is time to tell my
story.
I know it will hurt some. But in Helping others
in the process that will be my glory.
Even though at times it will hurt and feel like
purgatory.

I am not who I have been.
I have upgraded from hating myself and fearing
that toothy grin.
Turning a leaf, almost like I can be made more
beautiful as the darkness I trim.

I am breaking the secret. I did not agree to keep
this terrifying secret pact.
Flowing from my soul it is marked and blacked.
Cleaning the mess will take time, I will not get a
plaque.

However, I am not on my knees. I am shaky but
standing.
Love will not be my weakness again. I will
create my own landing.
I am still grieving a sweet girl slain for a man's
gain.
I am done trying to scrub and rub the dirtiness
and shame down the drain.

No, I am not who I used to be. I am trying to be
strong.
Blazing new ways, starting a new phase to find
where I belong.
Shining lights on parts of me that I had thought
were long since gone.

No, I cannot separate from the past.
It happened. I can only move forward and blaze
a new way.
Most days I am strong, vibrant even focused on
myself at last.
Other days I am overwhelmed by grief and by
anger.
But what I know for sure, I am not who I was
before.

The Monster Inside

I am so blue and sad. I think I may burst.
Am I really feeling this bad? Or am I just cursed.
The rage comes in and it crests. I always hate on
myself first.
A hot smolder to the point of obsess. Knowing I
let myself be coerced.
Coerced, intimidated into being silent. To
playing his sick game.
Always Teeming with violence. whipped and
tamed.
I carry too much of his load. Under pressure and
locked.
Always in survival mode. I am trying with all
my might to get it unblocked.
The slick monster, he still wants me. Might be
the only one who has.
He's hoping I run to him and flee. He wants to
possess me like they do in Alcatraz.
A prison surrounded by deep cold ocean water.
Death is the only way out, keeping me in my
place.
Letting no wounds be cautered. The punishment,
love never trusted, felt or embraced.
The only one who ever bothered. Only wants to
possess and destroy my soul.

Where was my father or my mother? They instead gave up parental control.
They let the dark in. He wants me to feed his sickness. An insatiable appetite he is unwilling to control.
He tries to avert suspicions with charming slickness. Showing off with his nice droll smirk.
I must let go to be free. I must let out what I allege.
I pause for a minute, to just be me. Making myself this pledge.
I will speak my story. I will shout it loud and high.
He deserves no glory. For he has ruined me by and by.
I climb up a mighty tall tree. I shout to heaven with an indignant cry
The wind fills my lung. A sweet but cold air exhales.
A treat of a late winter's day marked by a bright sun. Cold but still burning my skin, basking but too fair.
The truth, sure it burns and hurts sometimes.
But it beats the slow inevitable dying.
Please remember my rhymes. When you feel that someone is lying.
Pay attention before it is too late. Monsters have many faces.

Faces that are sweet and warm, some even with
a very handsome form. Please, do not let this be
your regret.
It tears me apart. Knowing that I could have
been saved.
If only someone had played their part. If only I
had been raised.
Now, It is my turn. To save others from paying
the same price.
The product of ignoring. I know too well the
burn and the fight. I keenly feel others sadness
and real regret and can see sad flickering lights
when they are in my sight.

My Hero

Her smile is beautiful and she is missing her two
front teeth.
Perfect in her imperfection.
She laughs out deep and loud like no one is
listening.
The soundtrack of her fiery soul.
No hand up to hide her smile or muffle the
sound.
She cares deeply about sweet candy and
ice-cream.
She will tell you all about it with a big chocolate
grin.
She may even offer you some.
She dances soulfully and big big like no one is
watching.
Dancing to the beat of her choosing.
Releases song notes without hesitation.
When she cuddles in so sweetly, she has no
worry in the world.
Until falling asleep in innocence and safety.
She rests so deeply with a carefree snore.
Oftentimes she wears bright princess dresses to
the store.
Sometimes in mismatched leggings and sequins.

Knowing she can transform into whatever she may like.
She runs and skips without the worry of falling.
She says how she feels.
But, does not when she does not want to.
Intuition in her beliefs and giving affections.
Trusting her own mind and body connection.
Sweet childhood of being unaware of others' expectations.
Before the world makes her feel she is wrong.
Before she will question existence.
Before judgement tries to change the breath in her lungs.
Before she is told she must please others before herself.
Yes, she is perfect imperfection.
Sweet loving and wild.
Flapping her wings in every direction.
May she always know I am in awe of her spirit.
May she always show me what it means to be….
Free.

The Dark Figure

The dark figure descended upon
my life one day, I was just a pawn.
The devil and the figure placed bets
What would a man do if offered a bite?
The dark figure, he owns the night.
My nightmares and fear take flight.
Dreams of crushed souls
And of a life so cold.
Terrifying hands grabbing
Sharp knives are stabbing.
The dark figure wants to lay claim
To my life and soul, the same.
Feeling like this is what he is owed.
For allowing such awful acts to unfold.
Black rolling smoke around my face
Taking up my whole space.
I cannot move, I am paralyzed in fear
My death could be very near.
The black figure lying in wait.
Waiting to take what is on the plate.
I yell out for someone to save me.
No one hears me; my words fall flat.
It is useless, the figure owns the night like a bat.
I fall into my shallow grave.
I am tired, I can no longer be brave.

Covered by the weight of the soil
I know my flesh has been swallowed.
I have been slowly decomposing while living
Always being the one giving.
The black figure knows me.
Knows too well he has the deed.
The deed to my soul.
He always has, like a miner and coal.
He comes for me.
And the man hands me over and flees.
A coward and always so mean.
Such betrayal is not unexpected.
I have never been protected.

Meant To....

Being a girl or a woman, we are told we are
meant to...
Meant to be beacons of purity's light.
Even when that attention does not feel quite
right.
Meant to be cute but not too pretty but also
quiet.
Even when there is cause to start a riot.
Meant to always be polite and courteous
Even though that means being nice to the
dirtiest.
Meant to always be accommodating and
hospitable
Even when that means danger is the participle.
Meant to be like a painting, seen but not heard
Now all these double standards are absurd.
Expected to be unique but all the same.
Even though that is an unwinnable game.
We need to teach our girls and ourselves we are
meant to...
Be bright, bold and funny
And it's okay to be quiet when our skies are not
sunny.
Meant to be genuinely ourselves

Instead of perfect porcelain dolls kept on shelves.
Meant to run, play, and get dirty.
And when the moment is right no strings attached flirty.
Meant to be wild golden sunshine and pick flowers
Not to sit and be silent for hours.
Meant to be bright and smart
And even let on that we also fart.
We are special in our own right.
Have the right to fight.
We produce life beyond ours.
Able to nourish and care, super powers.
We are strongest when harness this gift.
Even when it feels like it causes a rift.
A rift between what we want and what we must.
We can have both if only in ourself we place our trust.

Insomnia with Post Traumatic Distress

Every night there is a full staff meeting.
Attendees: Me, Myself, and I.
Every ticking second is misleading.
I lay down to try and rest my mind.
My little home in the big wide world is silent.
Not too quiet, I can hear the loud snoring, the
sighs.
They are sleeping. My sweet loves lie cozy and
quiet.
I am lying… eyes wide awake going over every
lie.
My mind, it races so fast I cannot catch it
I run clumsily behind it, weighed down by my
past.
There it is gone and unattached.
Overwhelm. My body aches, will the night pass
fast?
The events of my past take on a life of their
own.
The memories they are real and hopeless.
Everything is all broken and blown.
I look around, keeping my eyes open
My living room, my couch, my blanket.
I try to ground myself, nothing spoken.

I put on the fan and crank it.
Attempting to dissipate all that memory smoke
I feel a hand on my back, a big cold hand on my
shoulder
I shrink in the coolness and hum as I try not to
choke.
A loud booming voice says "I will hold her."
I try to push it out and forget it
I am activated, goosebumps all over my skin
Frozen stiff in panic, wandering, I let it.
I try hard to push aside where I have been.
I pull up my knees and silently cry.
Life has broken me and I have sinned.
Taking the blame, I want to die.
It would end all this agony and pain.
I wish for even a minute it would all go away.
I pray for amnesia, a way out of these memories
today.
All my healing work has been in vain.
Looking at the shame I know who is to blame.

Finally

I hold out my shaking hands
You reach back out gently and cradle my heart.
On your finger, I put on a shiny new wedding
band.
You say "till death do we part."
Waltzing down the aisle.
I am so proud of this day.
To my favorite memory this is filed.
I know with you I will always want to stay.
My best friend has become my husband.
My past has not always been sweet
But on my feet, I landed.
You offered me your love when I was empty
handed.
Without hesitation you took the role of lover,
dad, protector.
I am blessed to have had my life disbanded.
For only then did I become my own life director.
I choose you to be my one and only.
Or did fate choose us to be.
I had known too many men who were phonies.
I dreamed of you, but to find you was no
guarantee.
Remember dear our sweet babies first cry, laugh,
and steps.

Watching you courageously evolve from a man
to an even greater father.
Being with you these past years has been life
changing.
Emotional support and love beyond the stars and
farther.
Together finding new ways and paths by trail
blazing.
Loving you is the closest to heaven I have been.
I know that you will be there for us time and
time again.
Knowing you are in my corner; I can take the
bad on the chin.
Having someone who loves me for me, just
plain.
Loving you was unexpected but you are the
reason
Reason for love, laughter, frustration, and
greatest joy.

The Future

45

My plans are far and wide.
For the first time I am going ahead.
There are no rules to which I must abide.
I will not wish or wait to be dead.
Living will be my focus
And I will be trying to be whole instead
I will no longer care if anyone notices
The control will be in my hands
And never again in the hands of bad men.
I will be the captain of my own plans.
Never to be put into a captive pen again.
I will be free and vibrant
I choose what my path will be.
Along the ways, I can cry and vent.
Harnessing the power of me.
Loving the butterfly I have become.
Emerge from the cocoon brand new.
Finally feeling like a someone.
And being a lighter color blue
I will not need to enter a plea
Because I control the future me.